Girls with Guts!

The Road to Breaking Barriers and Bashing Records

Debbie Gonzales ☺ Illustrated by Rebecca Gibbon

Charlesbridge

CANCE

For John, whom I am most grateful to have in my corner.
All my love.—D. G.

For all the girls who were told that they couldn't.
—R. G.

Published by Charlesbridge
85 Main Street
Watertown, MA 02472
(617) 926-0329
www.charlesbridge.com

Library of Congress Cataloging-in-Publication Data
Names: Gonzales, Debbie, author. | Gibbon, Rebecca, illustrator.
Title: Girls with guts! : the road to breaking barriers & bashing records /
    Debbie Gonzales ; illustrated by Rebecca Gibbon.
Description: Watertown, MA : Charlesbridge, 2019.
Identifiers: LCCN 2017055933 | ISBN 9781580897471 (reinforced for library use)
    | ISBN 9781632895684 (ebook pdf) | ISBN 9781632895677 (ebook)
Subjects: LCSH: Sports for women—United States—History—Juvenile literature.
    | Sex discrimination in sports—United States—History—Juvenile literature.
    | United States. Education Amendments of 1972. Title IX—Juvenile literature.
Classification: LCC GV709.18.U6 G66 2018 | DDC 796.082—dc23 LC record
    available at https://lccn.loc.gov/2017055933

Printed in China
(hc) 10 9 8 7 6 5 4 3 2 1

Illustrations are painted in acrylic ink & colored pencil on acid-free cartridge paper
Display type set in Rabbits Dummy by Typetype
Text type set in Dante by The Monotype Corporation
Color separations by Colourscan Print Co Pte Ltd, Singapore
Printed by 1010 Printing International Limited in Huizhou, Guangdong, China
Production supervision by Brian G. Walker
Designed by Martha MacLeod Sikkema

Look at you . . .  springing,

 kicking,

dribbling,

and pitching it down the pike.

Girl, you are amazing!

It's hard to believe that there was a time when girls were not encouraged to play sports. It's true. Athletic programs funded by the US government were once for boys only. That was the rule.

Girls were told:

NO CHASING!
NO STRETCHING!
NO KICKING!
NO PUSHING!
NO SPLASHING!

And never, ever sweat.

Historically the boys-only rule goes way back to the early days of civilization. That's right: in ancient Greece, women were *executed* just for watching the early Olympic Games. *No girl competitors allowed. Men only.* Still, girls said, "Try and stop us," and they ran footraces in private festivals for Hera, queen of the gods.

Later, in 1896, during the first modern Olympic Games, female marathoner Melpomene made officials eat her dust. Denied the opportunity to compete, she defied the rules by running the entire race alongside the men. When refused entry onto the field for the final lap, Melpomene ran around the entire stadium instead.

The race to breaking barriers was under way.

People feared that active women would develop wild-eyed, jut-jawed "bicycle face," destroying their feminine appeal. In the late 1800s, Frances Willard challenged these and other Victorian beliefs by learning to ride a bike she named Gladys. Scandalous!

In 1892 basketball was a boys' game, considered too strenuous for tender girls.

But nothing stopped Senda Berenson Abbot from owning the court. A teacher at Smith College, Senda adapted the men's rules so daring girls could play. Their court was shorter. The rules were limiting. *No fast breaks! No bumping! Three bounces only!* And long bloomers were a must.

These pioneers competed when others said they shouldn't—or couldn't.

In 1909 polo-playing Eleanora Sears shocked society when she boldly
rode astride wearing pants—rather than a skirt—to compete in public!

In 1926 Gertrude Ederle became the first woman to swim the English Channel, soaking the notion that females were athletically inferior to men. Unashamed and self-assured, courageous female athletes pressed on, even when folks tried to squash their competitive spirit.

In 1928 Margaret Gisolo competed as the only girl on an American Legion junior baseball team. This fourteen-year-old's moxie made headlines. *Bunting! Sliding! Stealing! Beating the boys!*

Her team adored her. Her opponents deplored her.

"You don't belong here!" they shouted. *No girls allowed!*

Eventually, league directors barred Margaret—and any other girl—from playing as an American Legion junior. Still, female athletes kept coming on strong.

At age twelve Althea Gibson was a champion ping-pong player—the best in all of New York City! Then she traded her paddle for a tennis racket.

Althea dominated the court during the Civil Rights Movement. When blacks were struggling to gain equal rights in the US, Althea became the first athlete of color to win a Grand Slam title—smashing gender and racial discrimination lines by taking the French Open in 1956. Talk about guts!

Donna de Varona joined the 1960 Olympic team as the youngest swimmer, at age thirteen. Competitive, disciplined, and persistent, she bashed time-tested records and became known as the Most Outstanding Female Athlete in the World. Donna's future shone brighter than her gold medals!

Sadly, though, competitive swimming ended for this deserving athlete after four years on the Olympic team. Donna never made a collegiate heat sheet. If she wanted to swim in college and get an education, she would have to pay for it herself. At that time, athletic scholarships were for boys only. That was the law, and a barrier ripe and ready to be broken.

At the onset of the 1970s, valiant warriors came together to fight the unfairness.

Like any athlete worth her sweat, Congresswoman Edith Green stepped up to the plate to challenge athletic injustice. She teamed up with Shirley Chisholm, Patsy Mink, and scores of others who took a solid stand against educational, athletic, and financial discrimination with federal funds.

"Enough!" they said. "Equal rights for girls and boys!"

Game on!

Lawmakers debated.

Marches were organized.

The valiant fighters would not quit. They insisted that girls should not—and would not—be shut out from equal academic and athletic opportunities being allowed to boys only.

"Placing limits on the intellectual aspirations of women should be alien to the very basic concepts of this nation," Edith said. And she meant it. Discrimination was doomed.

Still, debates were held.

Hostilities were hurled.

After a long, grueling battle, a new law was passed in 1972.
Title IX mandated equal treatment for competitive girls. The law states:

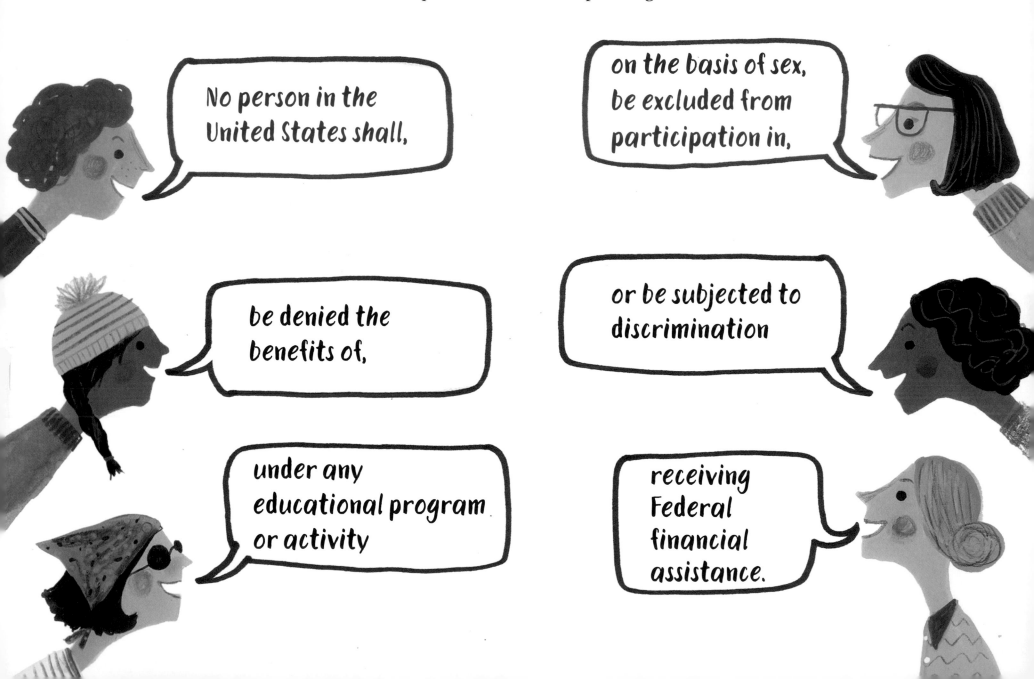

At long last girls had proper equipment, locker rooms, practice fields, and strong coaches for one and all. There was to be no more "boys only" favoritism under the federal law.

Yet the battle for equality raged on.

In the same year the law was passed, eleven-year-old Maria Pepe had pitched just three games before New Jersey Little League officials refused to let her continue competing with the boys. The New York Yankees said, "That's crazy! Why shouldn't girls play baseball?"

Officials believed the league developed qualities necessary for boys only. They thought fragile girls would get hurt.

Well, Judge Sylvia Pressler would not stand for it. She and others went toe-to-toe with the league and won. New Jersey became the first state to bar sex discrimination in Little League.

Eventually the majority of Little League chapters granted girls the right to play in either league-sanctioned baseball or softball games.

In time, female athletes began to experience equal treatment, changing the athletic world forever.

A new generation of female athletes dominated the 1996 Olympics. Team USA crushed opponents from all over the world and became known as national heroes. These women were deemed Title IX babies— triumphant female competitors born around the time the law was passed.

Thanks to Title IX, they were forever free to play like a girl at the Olympics and in professional, private, and academic leagues across the country!

It's hard to believe that there was a time when girls were not encouraged to play sports.

Today, thanks to gutsy girls and legends who changed history, you're free to stomp, jab, tackle, grind, and SWEAT. *Anything* you please.

Look at you . . . springing,

kicking,

dribbling,

and pitching it down the pike.

Girl, you are amazing!

Time Line

1880–1890

Bicycles become a craze in America. However, females are warned not to ride for fear of pelvic damage, spinal shock, and the development of "bicycle face"—marked by a protruding jaw, hardened facial muscles, wild staring eyes, and a strained expression.

1896

The first modern-day Olympic Games are held in Athens, Greece. Female athletes are forbidden to participate in any event, yet a woman named Melpomene runs the marathon course alongside the men, finishing in four hours and thirty minutes.

1912

"Can women be given access to all of the Olympic events? . . . Would such sports practiced by women constitute an edifying sight before crowds assembled for an Olympiad? We do not think such a claim can be made."
—Baron Pierre de Coubertin, founder of the modern Olympic Games

1918

Lauded as one of the leading all-around female athletes of the early 20th century, Eleanora Sears begins playing the game of squash. In addition to being a master competitor in polo, baseball, golf, field hockey, swimming, tennis, yachting, and speed-boat racing, Sears eventually becomes the first female national squash champion.

1925

As members of the women's division of the Chicago City Basketball League, the Roamer Girls—an African American basketball team—cross racial barriers when they compete against white and African American teams in the league and go on to achieve six undefeated seasons.

1880 1890 1900 1910 1920

1892

Senda Berenson Abbot adapts men's basketball rules for girls, calling for nine players on each team and confining each player to one-third of the court. Unlike in men's basketball, swatting the ball away from an opponent is an illegal move, and a game consists of two fifteen-minute halves, with a ten-minute break between.

1900

Despite lack of encouragement or promotion, a few females compete in tennis, golf, and archery during the Olympic Games. Golfer Margaret Ives Abbott is the first American female to win an Olympic event.

1900

The American Olympic Committee formally opposes women's athletic competition in all events other than floor exercises, during which competitors are required to wear long skirts.

1914

Alice Milliat organizes the FSFI—Federation Sportive Feminine Internationale, dedicated to the worldwide advancement of the serious female athlete. The FSFI holds the first Women's Olympic Games in Paris. Seventy-seven female athletes from five countries compete in javelin, shot put, running, and jumping events, as well as exhibition matches in basketball, gymnastics, and pushball, attracting more than 15,000 fans.

1922

"Gentlemen, if you attempt to do away with girls' basketball in Iowa, you'll be standing in the center of the track when the train runs over you!"
—John W. Agans, cofounder of the Iowa Girls High School Athletic Union

1925

1926

On August 6, Olympic champion and former world-record holder Gertrude Ederle swims the English Channel.

"People said women couldn't swim the Channel, but I proved them wrong."
—Gertrude Ederle, "Queen of the Waves"

1943

The All-American Girls Professional Baseball League is formed in efforts to keep baseball popular in the public eye while able-bodied men fight in World War II. To assure the highest standards of femininity, players attend charm school and are given beauty kits, complete with instructions for beneficial use.

1970

Congresswoman Edith Green initiates the first congressional hearings on education for women. She and her distinguished team present evidence that the lawful practice of excluding girls from educational opportunities on the basis of their sex is unjust and unconstitutional. These hearings serve as the starting block in the pursuit of female equality in the academic and athletic arenas.

"All I want and all I ask is that if two individuals, a man and a woman, come to a college or university and they have equal credentials and apply for admissions, that they be treated as equals."
—Congresswoman Edith Green

1972

Maria Pepe earns a spot on the Hoboken, New Jersey, Little League baseball team. After she pitches three games in regulation play, the parents of the opposing teams protest on the grounds that girls do not belong in Little League. League officials demand that Maria be dropped from the roster. Following media reports, the Yankees general manager honors her as an official Yankee of the Day.

1928

American Legion junior league baseball player Margaret Gisolo's case draws national attention in the *New York Times* and Movietone News. One newspaper stated that "the rules did not provide for girls to compete with boys."

1957

Althea Gibson is named Female Athlete of the Year by the Associated Press the year after becoming the first person of color to win a Grand Slam title (the French Open). Althea eventually goes on to win ten more Grand Slam titles.

"Shaking hands with the Queen of England was a long way from being forced to sit in the colored section of the bus going to downtown Wilmington, North Carolina."
—Althea Gibson, in reference to winning Wimbledon in 1957

1964

"That's what I'm here for—to get that gold medal, boy. It's freestyle. Gung ho. Guts out."
—Donna de Varona, Olympic swimmer, gold medalist in the 400-meter individual medley and 4x100-meter freestyle relay

1971

"We do not need that kind of character in our girls, the women of tomorrow."
—New Haven judge John Clark FitzGerald in his ruling against girls participating on boys' track teams

1971

Educational Amendments ban sex discrimination in education and Title IX is approved by the House of Representatives. The issues of girls, school, and sports move into the forefront. Lawmakers struggle with solutions to desegregate opportunities for female athletes.

1972

On June 23, President Richard Nixon signs Title IX and the Educational Amendments of 1972 into law.

Time Line

1991
The International Olympic Committee makes the historic decision stating that all new sports included in the program must feature a women's event.

1984
"Without Title IX, I'd be nowhere."
—Cheryl Miller, basketball player, 1984 Olympic gold medalist

1999
At the Women's World Cup, the US women's soccer team beats China in sudden-death overtime with a 5–4 penalty kick victory. The game is the most attended women's sports event in history, held in Pasadena's Rose Bowl before a sellout crowd of 90,125 fans. Goalkeeper Briana Scurry, defender Brandi Chastain, and the entire team become America's darlings and the first team to win the World Cup at home.

2012
For the first time in history, US female athletes win more medals than males—58 to 45—at the Olympic Games in London.

2016
In Rio, 61 of the 121 Olympic medals earned by the US team are awarded to female athletes, including Aly Raisman, captain of the "Final Five" women's gymnastics team. In the artistic gymnastics competition, the Final Five won the third team Olympic gold medal—the second on international soil.

"That's the beauty of the Olympics—the whole world comes together, united in their love for sports. I let myself have a moment to think about how momentous this was."
—Aly Raisman

"Before Title IX, one in twenty-seven girls played sports. Today that number is two in five. While we still have far to go before every girl has equal access to sports, especially girls of color, it is clear that we are making headway."
—Maegan Olmstead for the Women's Sports Foundation

1980   1990   2000   2010   2020

1989
Victoria Bruckner is the first girl to play in the Little League World Series. She covers first base, bats cleanup, and pitches in the final game.

1974
After a vicious battle involving the suspension of two thousand Little League team operations in protest, the New Jersey Superior Court rules in the girls' favor. Little League rules are revised to allow participation by girls. The Little League also creates a girls-only softball league.

1996
American female athletes—Title IX babies—dominate the Atlanta Olympic Games by winning gold medals in gymnastics, soccer, softball, basketball, track, swimming, and synchronized swimming. The gold medal soccer matchup between the USA and China takes place before a record-number 76,481 spectators—the largest crowd up to that time to attend a female sporting event. The USA wins in a celebrated 2–1 victory, yet there is no live coverage of the historic game.

2004
Forty percent of athletes participating in the Olympics are women.

2014
Mo'ne Davis, at age thirteen, is the first African American female to pitch in the Little League World Series. She pitches a shutout and earns a win. Mo'ne is one of two girls to compete in the 2014 World Series games and the first to appear as a Little Leaguer on the cover of *Sports Illustrated*.

2017
Tennis player Serena Williams secures number one world ranking by beating her sister, Venus, in the Australian Open. The victory earns her her twenty-third Grand Slam title—five more than the world's highest-ranking male player. Previously she twice delivered the "Serena Slam," winning all four major events in the same calendar year.

"Amazing things happen when you give female athletes the same funding as men."
—Donna de Varona, sportscaster and the first president of the Women's Sports Foundation

Author's Note

What does it really mean to "play like a girl"?

Does it mean that because females are sometimes viewed as inherently weak, little should be expected of them in the athletic arena? Hardly. Or, since sports have historically been a guy thing, girls can't be serious about participating? No, I don't think so. Neither would Senda Berenson Abbott, Gertrude Ederle, Edith Green, or the women who fought for Title IX.

I believe that female athletes share a common spirit, a sisterhood bound together by a love of sport and for one another. At the inner core of this collective spirit is a warm sense of camaraderie that defies the boundaries of time. Even though inequality issues such as salary caps, prize money, and media coverage are still being challenged today, history shows that when a girl wants to participate on an elite level, she's going to do so, whether folks like it or not. These competitors, as fierce as they might be, also understand that their achievements serve as inspiration to younger generations—encouraging girls to fulfill their dreams on and off the field.

Courageous female athletes of the past and present demonstrate that playing like a girl means you have to approach sports—and life—with confidence, commitment, and drive in order to achieve any worthy goal. It means remaining laser focused and performing at your peak level, no matter who deems the effort to be silly or useless. It means being aware that, when you excel in your sport, it's a win for all girls everywhere.

Ultimately to "play like a girl" means to dig deep, and then deeper, competing at one's utmost capacity while empowering others to do the same.

You go, girl!

Bibliography

"1999 FIFA Women's World Cup." *United States Soccer Federation*. Accessed February 18, 2017. https://tinyurl.com/ydf77x6f

Abrams, Douglas E. "The Twelve-Year-Old Girl's Lawsuit That Changed America: The Continuing Impact of *NOW vs. Little League Baseball, Inc.* at 40." *Virginia Journal of Social Policy and the Law* 20, no. 2 (2012): 241–269. http://scholarship.law.missouri.edu/facpubs/?utm_source=scholarship.law.missouri.edu/facpubs/506&utm_medium=PDF&utm_campaign=PDFCoverPages

"Althea." *PBS*, Public Broadcasting Service, 31 Aug. 2015, www.pbs.org/wnet/americanmasters/althea-althea-gibson-timeline/5393/

"Amazing Moments in Olympic History: 1996 Women's Soccer Team." Team USA, June 3, 2009. https://tinyurl.com/yasby3zo

Ashe, Arthur. *A Hard Road to Glory: A History of the African-American Athlete, 1919–1945*. New York: Warner, 1988.

Berg, Aimee. "Flash Back 20 Years to the Atlanta 1996 Olympics—When Women Reigned Supreme." *espnW.com*, July 20, 2016. https://tinyurl.com/yb3zfqly

Blumenthal, Karen. *Let Me Play: The Story of Title IX: The Law that Changed the Future of Girls in America*. New York: Atheneum Books for Young Readers, 2005.

———. "The Truth about Title IX." *The Daily Beast*, June 22, 2012. http://www.thedailybeast.com/articles/2012/06/22/the-truth-about-title-ix.html

Cahn, Susan K. *Coming on Strong: Gender and Sexuality in Twentieth-Century Women's Sport*. New York: Free Press, 1994.

Campbell, Terri, and Jennifer Tripp. "National Organization for Women." *Learning to Give*. Accessed May 12, 2015. http://www.learningtogive.org/resources/national-organization-women

"Chicago's Roamer Girls Were Pretty, Magnificent." Black Fives Foundation, December 11, 2007. http://www.blackfives.org/chicagos-roamer-girls-were-pretty-magnficient/

Crowe, Chris. *More Than a Game: Sports Literature for Young Adults*. Lanham, MD: Scarecrow, 2004.

"Games of the XXVIth Olympiad—1996." *USA Basketball*, September 12, 2014. https://tinyurl.com/y92248cq

Garcia, Patricia. "Women Won the Most Medals for Team USA at the Rio Olympics." *Vogue*, August 22, 2016. https://tinyurl.com/k2pspsv

"Gertrude Ederle." *Biography.com*, October 22, 2014. http://www.biography.com/people/gertrude-ederle-9284131

Gottesman, Jane. *Game Face: What Does a Female Athlete Look Like?* New York: Random House, 2001.

History.com Staff. "Althea Gibson." *History.com*, A&E Television Networks, 2009, www.history.com/topics/black-history/althea-gibson

"History of Women in Sports Timeline, Part 2: 1900–1929." *AAUW Lawrence County (NY) Branch*. Accessed January 19, 2017. http://stlawrence.aauw-nys.org/timelne2.htm

Isaacson, Melissa. "Small Wonders: The Girls Who Toppled Little League." *espnW.com*, August 11, 2014. https://tinyurl.com/notb5h5

———. "Small Wonders: Reliving the Fun That Never Was." *espnW.com*, June 30, 2014. https://tinyurl.com/nkdmdk3

"Key Dates in the History of Women in the Olympic Movement." *International Olympic Committee*. Accessed January 20, 2017. https://tinyurl.com/y7na5s3j

Leslie, Lisa. "Title IX: Lisa Leslie Is Proof Positive." *espnW.com*, March 26, 2012. https://tinyurl.com/yc9wb6dc

Leung, Rebecca. "The Battle Over Title IX: Male Athletes Suing to Change the Law." *CBSnews.com*, June 27, 2003. http://www.cbsnews.com/news/the-battle-over-title-ix/

"Margaret Gisolo." *National Italian American Sports Hall of Fame*, November 8, 2012. http://www.niashf.org/inductees/margaret-gisolo/

"Maria Pepe: Little League's First Girl." *Makers.com*. Accessed April 21, 2015. http://www.makers.com/maria-pepe

Markusen, Bruce. "Baseball History Filled with Women's History." *National Baseball Hall of Fame*. Accessed April 29, 2015. https://tinyurl.com/yaqcnd29

McDonagh, Eileen, and Laura Pappano. *Playing with the Boys: Why Separate Is Not Equal in Sports*. New York: Oxford University Press, 2008

"Most Tennis Grand Slam Titles Winners (Men & Women)." *Total Sportek*, January 28, 2017. http://www.totalsportek.com/tennis/grand-slam-titles-winners-mens-women/

Nat. Org. for Women v. Little League Baseball, Inc. 127 N.J. Super. 522, 318 A.2d 33 (1974). https://law.justia.com/cases/new-jersey/appellate-division-published/1974/127-n-j-super-522-0.html

O'Reilly, Jean, and Susan K. Cahn. *Women and Sports in the United States: A Documentary Reader*. Boston: Northeastern University Press, 2007.

"Our Name." *Gladys Bikes*. Accessed April 21, 2015. http://gladysbikes.com/whatwedo/

Parcina, Ivana, Violeta Siljak, Aleksandra Perovic, and Elena Plakona. "Women's World Games." *Physical Education and Sport Through the Centuries* 1, no. 2 (2014): 49–60. http://www.fiep-serbia.net/docs/vol-1-i-2/en/paper-5.pdf

Rappoport, Ken. *Ladies First: Women Athletes Who Made a Difference*. Atlanta: Peachtree, 2005.

Russo, Neal. "Girl Legion Star of 1928 Recalls Play for Blanford," 1958. Wabash Valley Visions & Voices Digital Memory Project. https://tinyurl.com/ybqctbdp

Singh, Kyli. "Here's What the 1996 Olympics U.S. Women's Gymnastics Team Looks Like Now." *Huffington Post*, August 4, 2016. https://tinyurl.com/ya3y4kdc

Suggs, Welch. *A Place on the Team: The Triumph and Tragedy of Title IX*. Princeton, NJ: Princeton University Press, 2005.

Times, The New York. "Althea Gibson, First Black Wimbledon Champion, Dies at 76." The New York Times, *The New York Times*, 28 Sept. 2003, https://www.nytimes.com/2003/09/28/obituaries/althea-gibson-first-black-wimbledon-champion-dies-at-76.html

Tierney, Mike. "A Novelty No Longer: Girls in Little League World Series Become Less of a Phenomenon." *New York Times*, August 13, 2014. https://tinyurl.com/ydxbq4va

"Williams Completes Historic 'Serena Slam.'" *Wimbledon.com*, July 11, 2015. https://tinyurl.com/ybav9mnl

"Women's Basketball Timeline—Since 1891." *Women's Hoops* (blog), June 25, 2012. https://womenshoopsblog.wordpress.com/womens-basketball-timeline-since-1891/